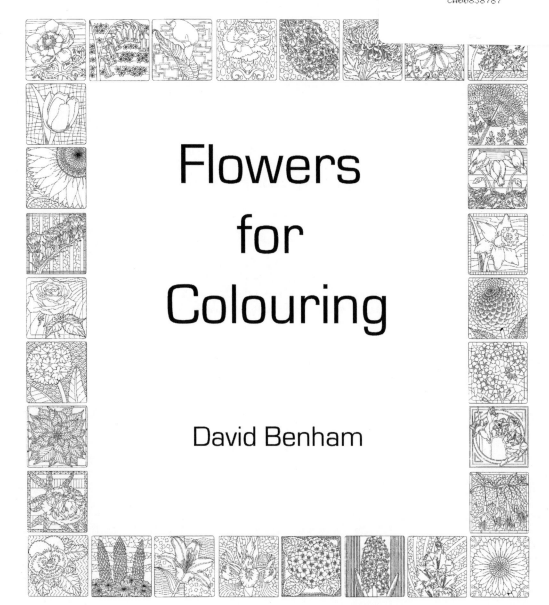

Flowers
for
Colouring

David Benham

Flowers for Colouring

Copyright © 2015 David Benham

ISBN-10: 1511970669
ISBN-13: 978-1511970662

www.davidbenham.co.uk

From the flamboyant bloom of a chrysanthemum
to the simple beauty of a forget-me-not,
flowers come in a huge variety of shapes, sizes and colours.
Now, with this inspiring collection of thirty original floral designs,
you can pick up those colouring pens or pencils
and let your creative imagination run riot.

This edition features the following flowers:

Anemone	Daffodil	Lily
Bluebell	Dahlia	Lupin
Calla Lily	Forget-me-not	Pansy
Carnation	Freesia	Peony
Cherry Blossom	Fuchsia	Poinsettia
Chrysanthemum	Gerbera	Primula
Clematis	Gladiolus	Rose
Cornflower	Hyacinth	Statice
Cow Parsley	Hydrangea	Sunflower
Cyclamen	Iris	Tulip

The back of each colouring page is blank
so that when your own unique work of art is finished,
it can be cut out and hung up for display if desired.

anemone

bluebell

calla lily

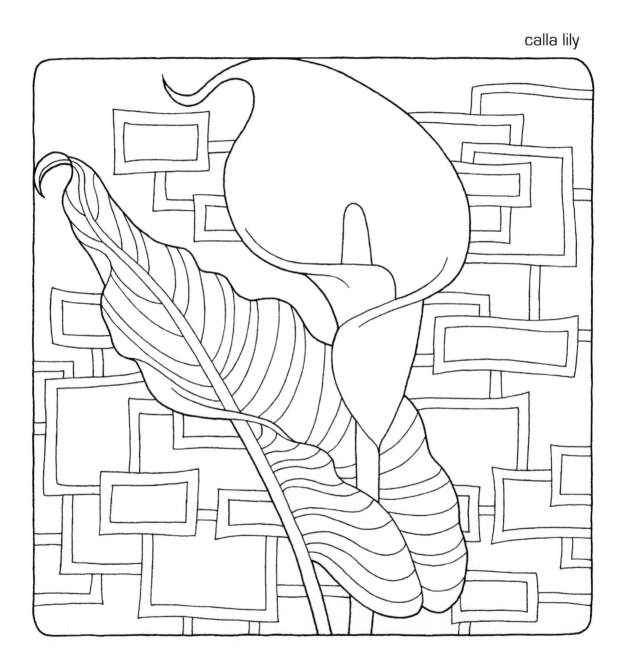

chrysanthemum

cyclamen

daffodil

dahlia

fuchsia

gerbera

hyacinth

hydrangea

lily

lupin

poinsettia

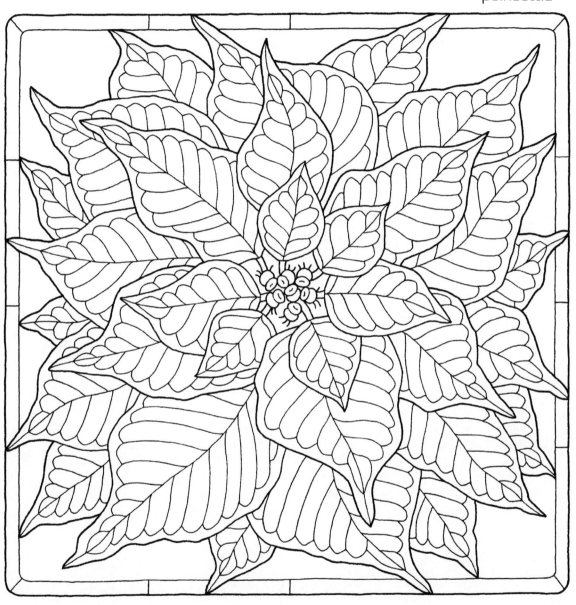

rose

statice

tulip

Printed in Great Britain
by Amazon.co.uk, Ltd.,
Marston Gate.